Bird's Eye View

By the same author:

Tribute Night at the Social

Whisper on the Shore

Pause and Rewind *(series)*

Connections : Railway Verses

Dedicated to my wife
and our family and friends
with love

Bird's Eye View

Peter Burgham

from Coast to Coast
in verse

First Printing: 2021
(Originally published in 2020 as *Burg's Eye View.*)

ISBN 978-1-9163353-8-7 (paperback)

ISBN 978-1-9163353-9-4 (e-book)

Published by: Peter Burgham
York, England

A CIP catalogue record for this book is available from the British Library.

Website: www.burg34.com

Front Cover: *Yorkshire coast (Filey)*
Back Cover: *Aletsch glacier at Jungfraujoch, Switzerland*

Contents

BAYCOMBE

BAYCOMBE

[A compendium of scenes set in and around my fictional English seaside resort, Baycombe.

Seaside resorts have a unique history and a special place in British tradition. They emerged in the 18th century as health and pleasure destinations for the wealthy, with their natural attractions of sandy beaches, rocky promontories, invigorating sea air and sea-bathing.

Man-made additions to the experience brought the now ubiquitous amusement arcades, funfairs and fish-and-chip shops. In particular, the advent of railways in Victorian times led to Blackpool becoming the world's first working-class seaside resort. Thousands flocked from the grimy industrial towns and cities for precious relaxation.

The heyday came in the 1950s and 1960s, when regular holidays became affordable to many people through paid annual leave. It became fashionable to spend time at the seaside, in places such as Scarborough, Morecambe, Whitby, Margate, Brighton, Llandudno, Rhyl, Southport, Torbay, Skegness, Weymouth, Largs, Ayr, Bognor Regis, Rothesay, Cleethorpes, New Brighton, Great Yarmouth, and so on.

In recent years there has been much decline, with consequent social and economic problems in some areas. But there are now signs of recovery and regeneration, with projects to study and preserve Britain's magnificent seafront heritage, and other initiatives to help these communities to prosper once more.]

Speed Dating in a Northern Town

Go ahead sing that note
you know the one
that soaring second
syllable
that perfect pitch
the dulcet cocktail of
citrus and Tuscan light
flushing away
the flat beer of
dull industrial
breeze-block.

Be not a glass half full
            nor a square peg
                        nor a patched-up doll

be not a collector of beer mats
            nor a stinging nettle
                        nor an ornament on a shelf

be not an icy wind
            nor a babbling stream
                        nor a rabbit in the headlights.

Enter that sun-kissed garden
find that celestial match
      vincerò
      vincerò
be my winner tonight.

A Stranger's Eyes

At the party
through the forest of
camouflaged faces

a butterfly
fragile
unassuming

lands
with a flutter
on a leaf
          the flit of a wing
          the glint of an eye
          the promise of the chase

          to net the prize
          be sure to take
          that simple forward pace.

All At Sea

The fish swims the bay
knowing only fish and water
and darkness. The fish

sees no shadows hears
no noise, never comprehends
the folly of the bait.

The fish out of water
is all at sea, a shadow
of itself, hooked.

Peach and Rose

(i) *To Be Beside the Seaside*

In casual conversation
on the tram in Blackpool
with two Scouse shopgirls wearing
purple glittered stetsons
on their way to a nuns' convention
got asked quite straight:

> *Hey, lar, who d'ya fink's da prettiest,*
> *me or me mate ?*

Throwaway camera to hand
I take a pretty mean snapshot
of the Tattoo'd Ladies
neatly framing as backdrop
the steel-faced pier-end
and a donkey's rear-end.
I smile, show the photo,
and slip myself out of the picture:

> *Ah, ladies, who knows*
> *how to choose between a peach and a rose?*

I check the watch, move towards the exit,
dodge the horticultural debate.

(ii) *The Razzmattaz*

All around, illusions:
The Bearded Lady *The Girl in Goldfish Bowl*
The Headless Mummy *The Eiffel Twin*

Roll up roll up to the culture-free zone
Neon lights and lasers pinned on mobile phone

Ride the rollercoasters all-day with your tag
Slide on into dumbdown all-night on a stag

Beat the Guinness Record for drinking from a shoe
Spew the lot the furthest and beat that record too.

(iii) *Postcard from the Fifties*

If you've ever been to Blackpool
And sat on top of a tram,
You'll know the simple pleasure
That charmed yer Dad and Mam.

If you've ever made a castle
And buried yer Dad in the sand,
You'll know the priceless treasure
Of bucket and spade in hand.

If you've ever tried the dodgems,
And chips wi' pot of tea,
You'll know the simple pleasure
Of being beside the sea.

If you've ever held your lover
And kissed together slow,
You'll know the simplest measure,
And all there is to know.

(iv) *Kiss-Me-Quick*

Walking past the painted facades
of the B&B's and glitzy arcades,
where cast-off Kiss-Me-Quick hats parade
and clumsy troupes of litter dance
with the ghosts of the old variety acts
uncharitably discarded from the central pier
kicked away like empty beercans down the street,
arriving at the station, the answer still unclear,
next time do you leave your brains in the
luggage rack, wallow in the nostalgia and tack,
or head off to some upmarket *gîte* in France
or *hacienda* in Spain where the sun shines
each day and the prunus persica grows,
well, lar, which one's it to be –
Southern Peach or Northern Rose ?

Distant Stars

You smiled so sweetly for the camera,
    but your eyes looked lost far away,
to you I was just a dumb warder,
    who'd locked up your image that day.

You stand there silent in that black-and-white still,
    no sign of any emotion,
easy to see now the need to fulfil
    your vision of Technicolor Motion.

Silver at Midnight

moonlight served chilled
across the midnight blue
white spray showering

against the pier, honeymoon
lovers splashing through
the cold November air

hugging and teasing
back to the half-empty
seafront hotel

warm bodies young fit eager
eyes sparkling bright
champagne kisses gushing softly

over strawberry lips rolling
around the fur of the tongue
delicate bubbles flirting floating

fizzing inside mouths
locked like limpets
rocking gently in rhythm

fingertips reaching reaching
moonlight glinting silver
across the naked sea.

Gold at Noon

fifty years later
huddled at the seaside café
golden memories of shimmering
moons and chilly promenades unfaded,
old moon's still there,
kisses too, vintage years even though
the ritual toast now is of a different kind
served warm with a lick of strawberry
jam and a sip of Tetley tea.

Where Sky and Lancashire and Water Met

[The tradition of 'Wakes Weeks' arose in the north of England and Scotland in the 19th century. Mills, factories and collieries would close for a week for maintenance work, allowing the workers to seek (unpaid) rest and relaxation. As each town took a different week from June to September, it facilitated a steady flow of pleasure-seekers to Blackpool, Morecambe, Southport and the other seaside resorts.

As well as the by now all-pervasive train, a popular mode of transport for small groups of co-workers in the early 20th century was the 'charabanc', an open-topped motor coach. Charabancs were noisy, bumpy, and poorly upholstered. They were used for annual day trips, often the highlight of the year for many workers who would diligently save up weekly for the opportunity to get away from their grimy industrial habitats.]

A charabanc ride to Blackpool, the 1920s, trilby hats and flat-caps *de rigueur*. Sunday best tarred with the smoke of Woodbines, a large canvas hood to unfurl in the event of rain, six crates of pale ale sanctioned by Mr Arkwright from the outing funds - for spiritual fulfilment, and a handy suspension for the boneshaker ride. A jaunty wave to the hapless womenfolk, arms folded in resignation, as the party crash-banged down the road. The wheels turned slowly but no-one minded - four hours of singalong interwoven with philosophical banter and booze.

Harry Turner led the ensemble, a face like a busted clog but the voice of a Caruso. Sid Weaver, tone-deaf and toothless, imitated a mating walrus in the chorus. Old Joe Young smoked his briar pipe. The Irish lad Seamus played a reel on his harmonica. As the great metal snail lumbered along, the squad were sitting ducks for 'Cheeky Charlie' Carter's volley of corny jokes. Whilst they were laughing, Charlie surreptitiously hid a bottle of ale. But 'Fast Freddie' Cooper knew his tricks, spotted him and swapped it for an empty one, with a wink to Old Joe.

The iron and brick of dark Mancunian cotton mills subsided to gentle fields of wheat and cattle. The beer and the jokes flowed like the river Ribble. It turned out nice again for little

Bobby Miller who kept himself amused with a symphony for silver spoon and tapping knee.

And on they rolled leaving a trail of discarded wrappers, cigarette butts and bottle tops – a roadside festival of litter. A twenty-first century eco-warrior would have seemed like an alien from Mars.

A stop halfway for scientific research at the Royal Oak where 'Colonel' Ken regaled them all with war stories about British victory in Flanders mud (some scoffed unkindly). Bert the foreman from the works fell asleep at the bar, to the great amusement of the lads in his crew. 'Mad Dog' downed a pint in one, urged on by Zulu chants. Bert slept on. Tommy tried to steal a kiss from the barmaid until her barman husband called time. And on they rolled into the sepia mist of seaside days out. The saloon bar on wheels moved slowly but the time flew like a Bugatti Royale ....

.... Fast forward to the 1980's, a hearse ride in Bury, black hats and black ties *de rigueur.* A cold rainy day, 'God's tears' as Grandma called it. As the mourners arrived they searched out familiar faces amongst those gathered under umbrellas at the ancient church, sealing precious memories with a hug and firm-clasped palms.

At the service, chorus lines of favourite old hymns chimed like solemn bells. The deep baritone of Eddie Turner warmed the chill air like a malt whisky. Reverend Carter gave the eulogy. They lowered the coffin slowly and steadily, taking care not to jolt Grandad's last ride. The rain pattered down on his plain wooden canopy, but they knew he wouldn't have minded, in the weeping mist where earth and wind and water met.

*** The title is a paraphrase of a line from Philip Larkin's 'The Whitsun Weddings'.*

Lest They Forget

It was a quiet evening in Baycombe
yesterday sitting by the fireside
listening to the music of the candles

a tealight symphony
of lavender and rose
harmony and counterpoint

as delicate as a Chopin nocturne
its fragrant melodies releasing
the serotonin and endorphins

carrying the mystical sound of
ylang ylang. A gentle breath of air

and a little sideways flicker
as if an invisible child had made
a birthday wish.

A few doors down an old woman
passed away. Lived alone
they said, in her nineties.

Husband died in the war, kept
herself to herself. Ellen they said,
or Helen maybe. Had a cat.

Welsh Dragon

It reminded me of Megan, calon a thân.
I bought it in Llandudno from a brassy
Scouse shopgirl, a princess in disguise
behind a devil-horn mask. Exiled herself to
Wales she said to get away from the tedium,
the paucity of opportunity, the desperation
of urban life.
                    Her words, softer in my translation,
were Saxon arrows thudding into a bullseye,
her prize a paradise of picture postcard views
candyfloss and slot machines on the pier.
Service with a smile as wide as an estuary,
but the dark circles under her eyes
a declaration of long dreary shifts with
snowglobes and fridge magnets, untold
          scores of late nights
          chasing the dragon.

*

She was Megan in the mirror,
the young Megan who'd carried her fire
from Wales to the silver city the bright lights
and promise of Liverpool, casting off the
tedium, the paucity, the desperation of a rural
backwater.
               The dragons have danced and
roared for Red Meg. She's rolled the dice, flown
by night to Vegas, targetted the glitz and gold.
These days she stacks supermarket shelves
and on Sundays drags her aching body to the
Pier Head to look out over the estuary.

Eyes as green as the green green grass,
all heart and fire, calon a thân
          like this cuddly toy
          the size of Wales.

Speed Dating in a Northern Town #2

Sitter: I see Mills & Boon & candlelit dinners.
Mover #1: I see mills & pills & Greggs for a pie.

*

Sitter: I see potholes full of water.
Mover #2: I see swimming pools for ducks.

*

Sitter: Abandoned buildings are cool places to visit.
Mover #3: My wasteland could be your Garden Festival.

*

Sitter: I collect beer mats.
Mover #4: I worship the Aztec God Quetzacoatl.

*

Sitter: Barbed wire, rusty railings, nettles and litter, broken glass, broken heart, broken & bitter.
Mover #5: Broken record ? ... Let Jesus be your DJ.

*

Sitter: What if the person of your dreams is here, if the chance of a lifetime is in this very room ?
Mover #6: That's a nice wedding dress you're wearing.

*

Mover #7: Hi ! I work in Retail. I live in...
Sitter: Hi, sorry to interrupt. Look we only have five minutes. Let's not waste it on routine talk about jobs and locations. We need a moment of truth. A barefoot moment. To feel the sand between your toes you need to shake off those everyday shoes. If we speak the truth then only the truth would break us apart.
Mover #7: Er.. oh yeah... er that's... er very true er...
Sitter: This is a chance to be honest, a chance to show your vulnerable side. We'll probably never meet again, so what have you got to lose ? Tell me then, if there was one thing you would change about yourself what would that be ?
Mover #7: Er well er... dunno really... er no... sorry...
Sitter: Ah well... so what did you say your job was ?
Mover #7: Ah yes I'm in Retail... shoe shop... no great shakes really...

*

Mover #8: Square peg.
Sitter: Round hole.

*

Sitter: One man's railway graffiti is another man's coming of age piece of art.

Mover #9: I run faster in blue light.

*

Mover #10: If I said you had a beautiful body ...

Sitter: Another red wine over here please. Quick.

*

Mover #11: Is this seat free ?

Sitter: Do you have any history of drug addiction, domestic abuse or mental instability ?
Are you gay, Muslim, transgender or do you have a problem with any of these ?
Are you vegan, vegetarian or just nuts ?
Have you ever been or are you currently involved in espionage, terrorist activity or genocide, or between the years 1932-45 were you involved in any way with Nazi Germany or the Axis powers ?
Are you a Manchester Utd supporter ?
Do you say 'bath' or 'barth', 'class' or 'clarss' ?
Ever put a ferret down yer trousers ?

Mover #11: Funny you should mention that, I did once audition for *Britain's Got Talent.*

*

Mover #12: You are the cat's eyes of my nocturnal quest.

Sitter: All roads lead to me, duck.

Turning the Tide

[Driving along one sunny day on the coast road heading for the beach at Baycombe, listening to the radio, the signal fluctuated, and I got a crosswire between two local radio stations, one holding a serious debate about the local economy and the other playing traditional folk songs.]

"Baycombe has one of the highest
rates of drunkenness and anti-social
behaviour in England..."
"...put him in the longboat till he's sober..."

"Teenage conception rates in
some parts of Baycombe are
three times the national average."
" ...oh don't deceive me, oh never leave me..."

"The smoking in pregnancy rate
is double the national average."
"...where have all the flowers gone?..."

"The transient nature of the
population leads to chronic problems
in housing and behaviour."
"...oh Maggie Maggie May they have taken her away..."

"People are living in bedsits without
running water or heat, some are sheltering
in tents in the sand dunes..."
"...this was the charter, the charter of the land..."

"On the positive side Baycombe is
a top place for entertainment."
"...oh you pig-tailed sailor hanging down behind..."

Popcorn

Popcorn on the pavement
Poster on the wall
Neon lights blaze stardom
Above the cinema hall.

Beercans in the gutter
Drunken locals brawl
Blue lights trapping shadows
Beyond the cinema hall.

City centre weekend
Phenobarbital
Busted lights hang jagged
Above the cinema hall.

Washed-out popband poster
Cold graffiti scrawl
Hope fades dark to alleys
Beyond the cinema wall.

Sawdust on the sidewalk
Writing on the wall
Broken inner city
No Superman to call.

Broken Promise

Those tears to me are imitation pearl,
Glass baubles manufactured on demand,
Costume jewellery for the drama queen.
A fashion show. A comedy. A performance,
Royal command.

And the nomination for the award,
For most deserving case,
Convinces no-one but yourself,
And falsely lights your face.

You curse your friends, your line, your luck,
You talk of LA, Rome and Singapore
But your words and schemes are like your gear,
Strewn wild across the floor.

In a world of tough decisions,
Your lies are where you hide,
Behind your cloak of virtue
Your secrets lost inside.

But when your promises are to children,
You expose your deepest fears,
Afraid to deal with honesty, or trust
Your own ability, or face the fleeing years.

And by your hands these promises
Discarded like cheap toys,
Theatrical props for the actress.
A puppet show. A parody. Another of your ploys.

The children do not understand
The excuses that you make,
They do not know the words for it
The liberty you take.

And they will not understand
This final senseless act,
Nor the wailing of the sirens,
Nor how they should react.

There is no pill I would not take,
No lie I would not swallow,
To bring you back here from the dark,
To rescue one tomorrow.

I used to think I understood,
Thought nothing of the pain.
Now the past is the future stolen,
And the truth is no-one's gain.

No tears of pearl run down my cheek,
But deep inside, a drama's played,
A cast of ghosts upon an empty stage.
A mystery. A tragedy. An endless masquerade.

Castles in the Air

Word-kites in the wind
the sandcastle promises
of barefaced hustlers

hot air balloons drift
above neglected streets where
politicians smile

hollow men who trade
their plastic trinkets for votes
mislabelling spades

Holding Forth – The Politician's Speech

In the hollow of the silence
at the drifting of his word
into the nowhere space beyond him
across the stillness
you could have heard
the beat of the wing of a wasp.

A breathless pause, noon in the desert
the spotlights unrelenting,
beads of sweat on his lips
he stood clinging to a prayer
his final sentence a smoke ring
suspended in mid-air.

Then came the single clap
like thunder to the fly
a second like a ripple
that echoed loud and more
then sprung by a cry, out poured
the well of emotion.

The storm of applause
and the standing ovation
the deluge of whistles and cheers
the doubts swept briskly away.
Acceptance. Relief. Votes.
A wave to the crowd, a gleaming smile.

The wasp saw his chance,
launched his campaign,
closed on his target elect
and without any scruples
got straight to the point,
politically correct.

Bird's Eye View

The seagull easy in his world
can't understand quite why
these humans cannot manage to do
a simple thing like fly.

The man stood on the edge of the cliff
gazing out at the distant horizon

trying to comprehend

    the vastness of the ocean
    the colour of the sand
    the purpose of the planets
    the lifelines on his hand

    the vanity of nations
    the labyrinth of laws
    the discord of religion
    the wilderness of wars

    the crumbling of the body
    the humbling of the brain
    the exodus of memory
    the darkness of his pain.

Or was he perhaps embracing the moment
a basejumper seeing it clear:

    blue skies, cool run, new gainer,
    dope cliff, no wind, good height,
    the beach, the vibe, no-brainer,
    front flip and keep it tight...

To the seagull on the shore below
that heard the raucous cry
the man was
as odd as an ostrich
as he stepped into the sky.

Whispers

if the wind was just ghosts
        calling

if the gust in the valley
        was the hwyl of honest men

if the dustbowl
        was the rebel yell of wasted youth

if the typhoons and hurricanes
        were the thunderous decibels of war

if the rustle in the trees
        was the muted cry of the long forgotten

if the whisper of the breeze
        was the desolate wail of the shackled and poor

if the leaves in the air
        were the tongues of wisdom

if we could decipher
        the language of the wind

Tower Block Grey

And then it's the last note of the day,
lights out and sack time,
when you creep through the semi-dark

the walls come closer and amplify
the scuttle of the night. Outside
you hear car doors slamming, angry voices,

a drunk kicking over a beer bottle crashing
like a glass tower shattering in a storm,
your fingers tensing at the rifle crack of

a creak from the outer door still not secured
since the last break-in. In the flat above, it starts,
the thud-thud of headboard on wall,

like the urgent clank of the engine
on a tramp steamer. Across the shaft of moonlight
intruding through the badly-fitting curtains

a mouse hurries, in civilian grey,
risking the searchlight to escape into its tunnel,
you wish it well on its secret mission.

Then it's Mad Mick again in the next flat
making his communion with his Wolf-God,
and you wonder how many moons circle his planet.

At last the distant silence of the walls.
No dripping tap or scratching mouse foot,
you wait for the thud-thud or crash of glass

to bring back your comfort zone of discomfort.
Sleep tight, my child,
tomorrow will bring light and birds singing.

You descend the tunnel to where
the mice in shades
sip cocktails on the beach.

Illuminations 2036

The war to end all wars
has ended

the stars have fled
the sky

day is night and the moon's
a burst balloon.

Bullets of black carbon rain
down on the ghost town

the dust of fairgrounds
and seaside hotels long forgotten

in a landscape from Mars
smoking eerily red.

THOSE EUROVISION NIGHTS

Amsterdam's Nachts

It's not what it seems the coffeeshop
Nor the snake house
Nor the drugstore
You don't go to the Red Light District
To buy a red light

The Van Gogh is not just Van Goghs
Everyone speaks English but they're actually
Dutch

Prinsengracht, Keizersgracht, Herengracht
Achtentachtig prachtige grachten
It's not people sneezing

There's no beach outside the Krasnapolsky
Despite the Hawaiian shirts and shorts

There's more canals than Birmingham
And chips with every imaginable sauce
Apart from Irn Bru-flavoured
But only a matter of time

Heineken is not just an Experience
It's a Rite of Passage.

The Couple Who Used to Own a Fireworks Factory

Paris. Eiffel. It was just by chance they met. He took
the first step. Polite, civilised, charming as ever.

He couldn't believe it, had it really been that long ?
They talked over dinner, candlelight, Beaujolais,

went onto the terrace to watch the fireworks display,
the choreographed ritual dance of dahlias and diadems,

peonies and horsetails. They remembered Venice,
the brocades and crossettes, the moon, the light breeze.

His eyes sparkled
and she missed the big orange flare.

Old Joke

A Canadian walks out of a bar.
Silence.
The silence of Saskatchewan.

Old adage:
Never explain your jokes
.... or your poems.

Add old age.
Silence.
No explanation.

Yeux Sans Frontières

Canada in Eurovision ?
Aussie Rules, mate.

København

Copenhagen International Airport, the signs
everywhere in English. Welcome to Denmark,
all part of the *hygge,* the warm comfortable feeling
of good food, good company, and good furniture.

Staff speaking perfect English at the hotel,
in the spirit of adventure, I switch on the TV to hear
some Danish. Instead, an episode of an American sitcom
and BBC News. Ah well, down to the bar for a Carlsberg.

Got talking, as you do, to a fellow traveller,
a cosmopolitan Dane as it turns out. It's all very cordial.
He tells me *I like to smoke wine and drink cigarettes,*
then pauses for effect: *chust my little linguistic joke.*

Went into town. Cold. Baltic. Warmed a bit to the train
announcement in English or is Danish getting so easy?
A brisk walk around this capital C city, no monuments
to kings or heroes, but a waterfront trophy of buildings
boldly plundered from an artistic raid on Amsterdam.

To get to know a place, you talk to the people:
the barmen, the taxi drivers, the maids and the managers,
the young and the old, the clean-cut and the bizarre,
smoke the wine, drink the cigarettes, eat the maps,
learn the language. *Ja. Ikke. Tak.*

People smile when you try. For the more advanced
situations, the phrase-book comes to the rescue:
I've forgotten my PIN sounding oddly
Scouse in translation.

And did I mention the beer ? And the furniture ?
They make very comfortable beds.
A sign hangs on the door:
Forstyr venligst ikke.
Danish. Probably.

Not Yet Twinned With

[If there was a Lonely Hearts Column for Towns & Cities…]

UNESCO World Heritage Centre in **Venice**
seeks
Like-minded UNESCO City of Music in **Katowice**

Folk singer in **Folkestone**
seeks
Limoncello drinker in **Limone**

Roman Aqueduct in **Montpellier**
seeks
Roman Gate in **Trier** (would consider Ampitheatre or Baths)

Escher puzzle in **The Hague**
seeks
Kafkaesque encounter in **Prague**

Salvador Dali Museum in **Figueres**
seeks
Salvador Dali etchings for crazy weekend in **Hyères**

Millennial in **Greenwich**
seeks
Clockmaker to pass the time in **Zürich**

Party advisor in **Vladikavkaz**
seeks
Advice on parties in **Graz**

Pub Crawl in **Glasgow**
seeks
Similar in **Krakow** (or anywhere really)

Eye Rhyme in **Marbella**
seeks
Time out in **Isola Bella**

Poles Apart

In the palm of your hand ripe
sweet but not for you Katia
you seal your lips translate
strawberries into designer wear
you bury your Economics degree
in the economics of hand-picking
in a corner of a foreign field
in Lincolnshire.

Ask her sister Anna the teacher who
cleans offices in Stoke if she
knows or cares if it's twinned
with Krakow or maybe Gdansk
for the benefit of trade
and cultural exchanges.

Ask the lawyer Pavel as he drives
his taxi guided by robotic command
around unfamiliar London streets
if he's familiar with the law
of the urban jungle, if he knows The Shard,
if he knows a good place to eat.

The glossy car adverts offer
augmented reality. The gangmasters
promise to keep the passports safe.
The taxi drivers and the warehousemen
learn new English words: agent, deduction,
welfare, mattress, sack, safe.

Back home, *mama* cooks *pierogi*,
tata counts the days. In a nearby country
they organise parades. In the flat fields
of the east lines of workers fill buckets.
To the north and south cold seas rise.
At Wimbledon they serve afternoon tea.

Parades in London

View from inside coffee shop, one winter evening

Boxed in darkness they wait like cattle
corralled into cold steel pens
by hard-line gangs, branded for steerage.
Swung by cranes, pitched and rolled
in transit to a distant shore. Shoe-horned
onto trucks. Offloaded without ceremony
into the hustle of the metropolis.

The fortunate ones make a statement
of a fashion. Landing on their feet
for an African's annual pay, they strut
the stage, do their Lambeth Walk.
For days they shine like costume jewellery
in a West End show, dream-porters,
coins tossed into a fountain.

Not all are chosen for the parade.
Wandering the back alleys like stray dogs
they fade into the shadows, rummaging
waste for a cast-off bone, or squat
cold in their square box of pavement
begging coins and muttering darkly,
they take their place in the order of things.

And the others, the in-betweeners, seeing
neither the darkness nor the light,
scuffing the surface, dragging their heels,
as unwanted as cigarette butts,
they're swept along, gutter junkies
jangling like empty tins,
as stateless as the wind.

View from inside coffee shop, one summer evening

Sitting at the window feet sore and hot
but invigorated by espresso, double-shot,
we play the old parlour game of guess the character
of the passers-by from what they choose to wear.

Armchair sleuths behind the shelter of the glass,
we size up the green pixies, the clogs & the slippers,
the brogues, the uggs & the purple winklepickers.
    -   what deep meaning should we imply ?

Hustle meets bustle - those two Mohican fashion
models holding hands walking proud
on stiletto are no ordinary models
for beards and heels are decidedly *outré*.

Pinstripes, shellsuits, bluejeans, blouses and burqas
hang from pegs on the cosmopolitan skyline,
as we box the chaos of tongues and skins
to instant order :
            bakers & bikers, teachers & preachers
            doctors & dockers, tailors & gaolers
            divas & divers, dancers & chancers.

Then a gaggle of rubber ducklings following the mother,
bright yellow T-shirts trooping their colours
behind a bobbing blue & brown umbrella
rubbernecking their big day in the big pond.

And hiding in plain sight behind the refugees
the politicians and the wheelers & dealers
      what shoes do terrorists wear these days ?
                    whose coat betrays the spy ?

Across the road, a tramp with tattered boots
slumps into his square box of pavement
muttering curses at the demons of time,
      and takes his place in the order of things.

Eating our cake, we're royalty, a king & queen
in modest disguise, amused by the passing parade,
the thousands now yet many more will pass in time,
but these are no big issues.

Practising for the Olympics

It's the only reason why
at 2:30 in the morning
you're pushing
your teenage son
down the residential street
on his skateboard
shouting encouragement

rousing the slumbering audience
from their suburban indifference
giving us the opportunity to say
we knew him before he was famous
he used to practise here you know.

To some maybe just
a bunch of drunken idiots.

From my bedroom window
I can see streets of gold,
I can see Britain's future.

The Lane to Nowhere

It awaits your exploration, the lane to nowhere,
beyond the uniform ranks of streetlights
and footsure pavements at the suburb's limit,
beyond imagined city walls.

The questions may outnumber the answers
but take your curiosity for a walk,
trek the clodden earth and wooded slope,
attain the ridge, dip into the pool of life.

Embrace the change, ditch sofa and fridge
for spade and boot, swap computer game
for compass, remote control for outdoor camp,
feel the icy edge of wind, seek out your root.

Go down the lane to nowhere
and plant a sign at somewhere.

*

Across the border the lane to nowhere
permits no questions asked, unmarked
past concrete walls, an icy wind swirls around
uniform ranks of lights that guard

the outer limit *for the safety of all citizens.*
The centre embraces all - the towns, farms, churches,
the outdoor camps - with its remote control machine.
The tannoy announces that everything is secure.

With worn-out boots and home-made tools,
committed camp-mates claw the rocky earth
to seek out the route to change the game,
but sensors blockade every channel.

At the end of the lane to nowhere
the lost supply the sign.

The Collector of Smiles

Crystal-blue flash
across the crowded *masserria*

shutter doors flung open
framing the image-queen

the debutante
exquisitely poised

a flutter of yellow chiffon
edged with black lace

chrysalis opening to light
an *ingénue* flirting with the lens.

His timing was impeccable, the suavity
of the raconteur, the velvet ease of years

photographing the beautiful. They talked
over *canapés* and cocktails, his voice

deep and jewelled, her laughter sparkling
as she tasted the salmon crostini,

prosciutto and melon, the nectar of champagne.
They danced to an orchestra of oleanders,

the citrus hint of his eau-de-cologne,
his whispered words a masterclass.

Hang-Gliding

A beautiful Swiss day in June,
cumulus clouds flat-edged, perfect
hang-gliding weather.

She's all kitted out, ready to go,
her eyes blue-green, her smile soft-curled,
this one takes your breath away,

and all she asks is that you hug her close,
step out from the ridge of the mountain
seek with her the thermal

where the golden eagles glide
with inherited ease
in the quiet of the cantons,

the one who says
        we can do this
        together
        we can fly.

Stretched out before you, the immense
Alps, the gilt-framed canvas,
vapours drifting into questions

how edges form and blur,
what passes for gold, why wings
fail short of the sun,

the one about sailing the clouds,
forever hanging in the twisted
tangle of your answer.

Academic Briefing

Redfin snappers and royal blue tang
paraded in choreographed formations
behind seahorses strutting centre stage,
        the flamenco school
        of the pelagic seas.

Above footlights of coral softening rockedges
glass minnows swirled and curved
in a silver pageant of mirrors & eyes,
        cast on the pin
        of his lens.

Snorkelling side by side they watched
a pair of mating jellyfish
drifting by in gentle embrace
        past the spawning grounds
        of the rainbow wrasse.

He taught her well:
to identify the types of algae
to spot the cuttlefish and the scorpionfish
        camouflaged against the rock
        when to touch, when not to touch.

Later that night surfing the photographs
he told her about the asteroidea and echinoidea
explained how the zooxanthellae
        gave the coral its colour
        their loss the bleach.

As they curled together on the sofa
browsing the cephalopods and medusozoa
his eyes were attracted to
        a perfect formation
        of charming white halfmoons.

She smiled coy as a nymph.
Cuttlefish and scorpionfish swam into view
and in the darkness of the Mediterranean bay
        Spanish dancers hid in crevices
        waiting for the dawn.

Baltic Echo

Ice packed deep in vaults
Beneath the wailing
Siren of the north, cold as steel,
Groaning an unheeded warning
Drowned by the violins
And clarion song
Of those no longer in peril
In the unforgiving
Mass of black
Where dark and still
She lay,
The broken hull.

Go now, rise up,
Like the birds
No longer awaiting the signal
That none knew but all would obey,
On the wings of salvation
Disturbing the morning air
Break out
Set free your heavy heart.

Kölner Wasser

Carnival time in the holy city
Offering its ode to the romantics
Locking their hearts into the steel green
Over the Rhein, inspired by the Dom's
Gothic grandeur, anointed with Kölsch,
No scent sweeter than the fabled
Eau. Word is, #it's_the_top_banana.

A Dream of Willow and Long Innings

A cricket-perfect sunny day in Bergen harbour,
the ship idling like a floating palace,
passengers lounging on the pool deck, sipping
Madras Sunsets served by Ajay with a smile,
the timeless forests and mountains over the Bryggen

hung like trophies inside digital cameras. A pleasant
warm breeze flips the pages of the guidebook back
to the Viking village hidden under the canvas
of modern city design: young men hunting, scavenging,
trapping bears, women cooking, weaving, ropemaking.

A rough life, cesspit, wattle and thatch, the daily slaughter
of pigs, goats, geese and cattle. Down at the water's edge,
battle-weary warriors returning with tales and trinkets,
the mission ended, oars at rest, mourners wailing at
funeral pyres, elders praying to the gods.

*

Images blurring. Many faces in the distance,
the long lens picks out women cooking,
weaving rope baskets, a wizened old man
sitting cross-legged deep in meditation, at one
with goats and cows, elephants, snakes, and monkeys.

A sudden swirl of moist air across wattle and pit,
ecstatic mothers lavishing hugs on cherished sons
home from sea voyages, wages thin as the weary
smiles left in transient pixels on the lido,
prized as the gold of the maharajahs.

Pandemonium of tuk-tuks and Mercs. A new dawn
carrying mobile phone chatter across India.
The clamour for wealth, for education and sanitation.
The rallying sound of dhol drums. Whistles.
A dream of willow and long innings. Cocktails with ice.

Yorkgate

Gate the Good

Congregate - Mitigate - Investigate
Delegate - Surrogate - Fumigate

Gate the Bad

Relegate - Tailgate - Profligate
Floodgate - Litigate - Arrogate

Gate the Ugly

Subjugate - Segregate
Castigate - Interrogate - Watergate

Gate the Mad (Gate loses the Plot)

Winegate - Bloodgate - Camillagate
Hackgate - Plebgate - Gategate
Make-it-up-as-you-go-along-gate

Gate around York

Stonegate - Micklegate - Coppergate - Fossgate
Monkgate - Castlegate - Skeldergate - Ousegate
Swinegate - Gillygate - Petergate - Nessgate

Gate goes Mad in York

Whip-ma-whop-ma-gate - Shambles

Gate goes to London

Moorgate - Aldgate - Highgate
Ludgate - Bishopsgate - Billingsgate

Gate on Tour

Harrogate - Navigate - Airport Gate - India Gate
Menin Gate - Brandenburg Gate - Golden Gate
Arc de Triomphe

Gate rests

Heaven's Gate

Moorland

On heathered moors we stood and gazed
at purple clouds that spoke of change,
as mad-eyed sheep scratched low for buds

beneath the cinders of a careless scorch,
and the kuks and quaas of startled birds
disturbed the slumber of the woods.

Burnt embers whispered to the alder darkly
in silhouette like a scarecrow starkly on grey
trapped in the bonfire of a reckless match

tossed into the tinder like urban trash
by day-trippers on unfamiliar ground
blazing their cross on an ancient map.

No hazels of wisdom found nor mystic wand
of Druid's yew, no sprig of rowan to protect
the elder grove stained red by wrecking torch

of firedragons that smoked the bees
from the honeycomb, felled English oak
and coppice broom and swelled unchecked

from Cornish tor to the sacred trees of Ynys Môn
bled Yorkshire heath and Highland glen
and seared the heart of Antrim's fairy thorn.

Across this island nation once more torn
the moorland sisters mourned the wasted bells
whose scent would never grace the breeze again.

Anno Domini

On the side of a hill in Bannockpace
there's a beautiful but awkward place
where the scent of the valley of purple heather
is mist to those here gathered together

where rabbits in their innocence
infringe our most instinctive sense
where a bird can lie with wing half-torn
unheard from dusk till early morn

where the wind cries out for a sleeping nation
and the flowers weep in desperation
where the headstones bow in sympathy
and life is put simple:

Born/Died <year> A.D.

Sorrento Seagulls

Quell'uomo -
Strano come uno struzzo *

* ostrich

SOUNDBITE CITY NEWS

Good Evening Britain

3-2-1 and cue Robert...
The Headlines Tonight (18 seconds):
Rainforest scam - Pope's visit to Iraq - President's
Blunder - More job losses - Major drugs haul.
No interesting deaths, an ordinary day.

...Silky smooth the anchor
Polished as a corporate banker...

Roll... Amazon rainforest - video of burning trees
(14 seconds)... sound's gone... ok, cut to Pope
And... cue Pope - live link to reporter - 10 secs - segue to
President's after-dinner gaffe... damn lost visual...
Ok, give me something, Robert...

...With suavity and style
He beams his trademark smile...

And in other news...
A traffic warden has been abducted by aliens.
Witnesses claim to have seen smiling green faces.
Sleep well, Soundbite City.
3-2-1 and roll credits. Adverts.

Instead

[There are at least 50 countries plagued with landmines. It is estimated that there are over 100 million in the ground, with exact locations unknown. There is apparently a similar amount in stockpiles, and yet production continues in several countries.]

If only each one were a peach instead
or a bowl of rice, or a sip of water, or a lick of bread.
If only each one were a tree, or a bee, or a bird in flight,
a red rose, or a gold coin, or a shining white knight.
If only instead the smile of a child,
or a dip in a cool mountain stream,
a wake-up kiss from an angel's lips,
or the end of a terrifying dream.

If only each one were a dud, a reject batch
offloaded by a silver-smooth salesman,
too slippery to catch.
If only the factories were moved to Mars
or all they made were chocolate bars.
If only the clearing of evil
could be done with one Superhero feat,
an episode of a makeover special,
instead of a hundred years on repeat.

One step at a time is the order.
Governments know the deal,
yet this is one border
they won't cross.

If only instead.
If only never works, sinks without trace.
and that is why now
in this God-forsaken place,
even the angels fear to tread.

Butterfly

[Some landmines have been deliberately manufactured in bright colours, shaped like butterflies, to attract children.]

Butterfly, butterfly,
patterned so bright
one touch of your wing
and we're all blown to sh***.

Lonely Planet

[Polar glaciers are melting at a dramatic rate.]

Along the dry river-bed teeming with dust
blown in from the Sahara
shrouding the bones of long-dead creatures
under the blaze of the unmasked sun,
a solitary traveller leads his camel
trailing silent silhouettes
through the riverbanks of dunes
towards the last ancient trading place.

In the distance, a silver lake reflecting sky,
quickening the step of the man
turning his world upside down
until its vanishing undelivers him,
cursing the shadow of the camel,
and somewhere deep in the ultrasound
beyond the still point, the desert
echoes to the shrieks of macaws.

City Workers

[Stress-related absence from work is at an all-time high.]

Regular beat down the outside lane,
Radio tuned to the local station,
A wake-up blast of vocals and horns,
City traffic jamming on cue in the rain,
Minds into neutral at the breaking of dawn,
Another working day for the rising nation.

... prospects in the pipeline,
mustn't miss the deadline...
... prospects in the pipeline,
mustn't miss the deadline...

Arriving at the office, ready for leaving,
Coffee-machine for instant relief,
Sugarloaf mountains of urgent reports,
Constant reminders of underachieving,
Numbers to crunch, obsession with noughts,
Walking the talk of corporate belief.

... need the win mentality,
cashflow is reality...
... need the win mentality,
cashflow is reality...

Lunchtime jostle a sandwich away,
Others pump iron for thirty non-stop,
Back to the bench to roll out the dollar,
Clock-watchers signal the end of the day,
Queuing again, hot under the collar,
Homeward to the thump of formula pop.

The Putter-Togetherers

["We are but two halves of a pair of scissors, when apart...but together we are something." Charles Dickens]

Forged in Sheffield steel these men,
hardened and honed by time-served drill,
proud of apprenticeships fostered
in the bulging pockets of boilersuits,
masters of the art, dark sorcerers of the put.

Precise to ten-thou's, nailing the swivel,
grinding curves to the cutting point,
craft refined through years of graft and mill,
hammer handles worn to their keeper's grip,
blue-collar knights of the pivoted steel.

Men who call a blade a blade,
no fancy titles for these stoic Yorkshiremen,
retirement long overdue, a dirty word
whispered in the corners of the noisy workshop,
unthinkable for the last of the putter-togetherers.

At home, wives, goddesses tempered on plinths,
perennial wizards in the kitchen and clothes shop,
deft hands turning copper to gold,
first amongst the putter-togetherers,
women who know the price of a pair of scissors.

Camomile Tea

[A small breakthrough into understanding the causes of amnesia is announced.]

It happened overnight, out of nowhere.
The doctors were puzzled. It was many months
before we saw you again in the office,
light duties. You'd sit quietly at your old desk

like a stranger on a train gazing out of the window.
You'd pass invoices to Jean in Accounts and fix
her printer. You'd do crosswords at lunchtime
and talk to Dave about the weather.

Whenever we passed in the corridor I'd say hello,
you'd stare for just a moment as if
trying to fathom a shape in the shadows
then you'd potter along to file statements.

As winter deepened, we yearned for a sight
of the first snowdrops. Plucky little soldiers
venturing out on patrol risking
ambush from the morning frost.

That day when Kev forgot his wallet and
quipped: *'I'll forget my own name next'*
we caught our breath, but you smiled,
a thin smile, the first shoot of spring.

And when the auditor made her annual visit
you remembered her name, you remembered
she liked camomile tea, you chatted about herbs,
the dew sparkled on the quivering grass.

But then out of nowhere your mind got lost
in the fog and you didn't turn up for work.
Jean rang, but your answer
was like a paper fluttering in the wind.

We wait for the snowdrops, John,
we file documents, we tidy our desks.

The Rose of Bhagranapur

[A famous and beautiful English actress receives an award for her unselfish charity work in India.]

She moves with grace but no airs,
Her gaze unflinching at the sight
Of the unblinking around her.
An English rose in a foreign soil,
Her delicate scent crossing distant borders
Far from the garden parties
And international movie premières,

Her smile the innocence of the girl within,
Soft as petals, natural as sunlight,
But the gold crown of neatly coiffured hair
An emblem of a different kind
For those wanting to unearth a darker story,
False rose, parasite, the succour
A deception to the world's unceasing eyes.

Study the classic composure, steadfastly
Borne through centuries of weathered storms,
On her spiritual journey beyond the Champs-Élysées
To the place of the living dead hereby judged worthy,
A primetime showcase for the outcast poor,
A bitter-sweet victory, the hard-won main prize.

Sopwith Camel

[Tales of heroism and courage emerged amidst the dark tragedy of World War I. The exploits of the Royal Flying Corps pilots were famously described in the series of Biggles books by Capt W.E. Johns. A handful of WWI aircraft remain in air-worthy condition]

The woodcutter carves and refines,
skilled with a plane, sketches the flight
sergeant's oily cloth, makes the wings rock,
lets the novice's undercarriage
bounce on the bumpy terrain,
maps out the foreign land of
fuselage, strut and chock.

A treasure chest of offcuts
on the floor of every page,
mysterious words and well-turned
phrases strung gracefully like
a staffel of Fokkers in flight,
an age of new vocabulary sweet as
chocolate on the tongue.

The books have gone west now,
collectors' items bar none,
a target for the nouveau correctness,
the bombastic smokescreen,
unloading all their eggs on the whisky
and the Hun, condemning the innocence
by wanting it clean.

Onward the campaign –
to defend the nation's flowerbeds,
to strafe the trenches of the duly elected,
dog-fight with the brass-hats,
make mincemeat of the dunderheads,
and salute the Captain
flying into the sunset, duly respected.

The 49th Sortie

[A service was held in Bannockpace to commemorate wartime air crew casualties, 75 years after the end of World War II.]

Heading out in the pre-dawn,
low overcast, no horizon, a factory crate
loaded with fuel and ammo to the max,
fabricated with scrap metal ingenuity
by a ministry in its darkest hours,
airspeed check, altitude check, wings level check,
cold miles trailing in the slipstream

the gnarled old hunting bird flies
in pursuit of a breakfast of
railway siding, oil refinery, unwary
trucks worming along the coast,
the dead-eye to guide the strike,
mindful of fuel, orientation, knots
and iron-fisted retribution.

The chilling intrusion of an amber light,
airspeed check, altitude check, discipline
on auto-pilot at the flicker of a threat,
sharpening focus for menace at every o'clock,
the weary bird heaves upwards
and settles once more to its mission,
low overcast, no horizon, *alles in Ordnung.*

Mersey Royals

["Life goes on day after day..."]

A duet in E flat for horn and seagulls,
mournful notes across the silt, an evensong
for the last in line of the Mersey monarchy.

Fragile circumstance and faded pomp
unfurled with undiminished pride. The ancient
right of passage of man and horse

ordained by royal charter, a ferry tale,
a commoners' tale of humble service
recounted from Domesday to Zeebrugge.

Steam power taming tide and time until
the tunnel vision of rail and road
brought its unrelenting storm.

Sunset over the river, gone now
the *Egremont* and the *Leasowe*, the legacy
reduced to dim-lit memories and economic debate

the famous *Royal Iris* rocked into legend
long since abandoned and dying alone,
the chords a distant echo, beyond resurrection

in rust-wracked dereliction,
not worth the tuppence to cross,
sinking like a flower made of stone.

The *Woodchurch, Overchurch* & *Royal Daffodil*
waltzing with the elegant guests of the Cunard
and White Star lines on the floating dancefloor.

A salute in unison on the shoreline from their escorts,
Seacombe a parade of primrose yellow, Woodside a jive
of blue-and-cream. New Brighton the handsomest of all

the Prince Charming of resorts with its sunlight smile,
the crowds in tribute with their buckets & spades
their model boats & their sandcastle flags.

Crown jewels of the Pier Head, the last two
dowager queens host the last great ball, an open
invitation for all the world to join the party.

High above the celebrated waterfront
the anchored birds
gaze across to Shanghai and New York
and offer their fabled blessing and protection

keeping afloat the heritage
and the vision of the city where
always in the centre of the dream
a magnolia blazes with light.

A Million Suns

[In 1990, the Marie Curie charity in conjunction with Liverpool City Council planted a million daffodils in Sefton Park, and named it 'The Field of Hope'. The idea spread, and throughout the UK there are now many 'Fields of Hope'.]

They've bulbed a million suns
in the grass of Sefton Park
assembled, primed, and classified
a weapon of mass construction
an army of the heart.

Hear then this call to alms
let it trigger just one spark
one flicker of hope or foolish pride
this solar-powered beacon
this natural work of art.

For here is no artificial invention, here is
    a flotilla of sou'westered volunteers

in a sea of green, a procession of torches
    fisting defiance at unwelcome invaders

a legion of heroes on the march
    a flash-flood of hazard warning lights

an exaltation of church bells ringing
    a fanfare of golden trumpets singing
    loud as smiles

rank after rank of New York cabs
    canaries fluttering and dancing

ballerinas *en pas de valse*
    Easter bonnets tipping at the trees

the periscopes of children's submarines
    swan-necks basking in the breeze

the swaying flags of the Brazilian nation
    a golden wave of Beatlemania inspiring
    the fab generation

they are the windmills of your imagination
        they are the fur of yellow cats.

For these are not just stems of flowers
to be picked by passing girls
chewing gum and junking pills
who chide

    What difference does it make, eh lar ?

We should ask old Billy
sitting
beside the lake

how easily we hide
how we can all become

lost
in the crowd

amongst the ghosts
of stolen daffodils.

Perfect Delivery

[Advocates of Road Transport are seeking further government subsidies.]

'*Perfect Delivery*' was the lorry's loud boast,
the crates of wine no doubt travelling well

although maybe a wee jolt or two as they pass
the disused land in Motherwell with its eerie call,

its voices lost in time, but let us not worry,
for the delivery will be perfect, ready for our weekly

shopping foray, and here's another convoy of
big-tonners hurtling along on the motorway,

like some wacky race to deliver the sofa,
the mock pine table, and the matching bookcase.

Phone them up, tell them how well he's driving today,
no matter that the destination is the other way,

from the Bannockpace factory to the Birmingham hub,
then all the way back to the Bannockpace shop,

aye, there's the rub. But hubs mean efficiency,
squawked the official parrot.

Others might say the transport industry
is going round in circles.

To the conspiracy theorists
it's all a fiendish plot.

Stephenson's Rocket

It was history served on a plate, its vintage glory
signalled on the up, a much-heralded arrival,
its preservation a triumph over every rival,
a strike of the gong heard from Beattock to Adlestrop
announcing Museum as the next station stop,
where well-versed stewards will safeguard the story.

Black-blooded aristocracy on the York outer ring,
streamlined and peerless in its model design
the very definition of *X Factor* in 1829
when *Downton Abbey* was the future sought,
and the *Tay Bridge Disaster* wasn't even a thought,
its fame is its ticket to ride like a king.

The weight of antiquity on a rickety old flatbed
rolling to a timetable nationwide planned,
en route towards its ancestral stand
to join the *Mallard*, the *Bullet* and the *Flying Scotsman*
and shunt the black sheep of the railway clan
the *Class 31* diesels to the sidings shed.

Resplendent and dapper, its chimney iconic,
an infusion of class on a diesel-dull Tuesday,
this mythical apparition evoking a ghost play
of top hats and tails in a school-textbook scene
where crowds rushed to touch the sleek new machine
(apart from one whose brush with history was sadly ironic).

But then from magic to tragic befitting Harry Potter
came the spike in the rail, the muggledom truth,
the googled discovery of iron-clad proof,
plainly this wasn't *The Legend* in view
but the *Baycombe Belle* a lesser marque from Crewe
yet gripping enough to hook the trainspotter.

Now to history buffs poring over vestiges of a Roman scene,
there's an aura around the ancient core of York,
so no surprise when yesterday eagle-eyed as a hawk
I saw perched on a car transporter in the traffic queue
the 1969 Mini Coopers, the red, white and blue
from *The Italian Job* - stuck behind a tractor on the A19.

Caught Smiling on the Underground

[A man was caught smiling on the Underground today. Police would like to interview any of the following witnesses...]

the overburdened magistrate who's had a trying day
the unemployed ventriloquist with nothing much to say

the drunken mathematician who's lost count of the bars
the overpaid astrologer who counts her lucky stars

the dieting diamond dealer who thought he'd lost a stone
the loudly-dressed librarian who's lost her quiet zone

the poker-playing pirate with his cards close to his chest
the lazy mattress inspector who goes to work for a rest

the artful little dodger who's heedless of the fine
the artless fortune teller who's looking for a sign

the brassy blonde cross-dresser who's BBC fake news
the trumpet-playing detective whose clues are in the blues

the sad girl from the chip-shop with the badly battered soul
the Premier League top scorer whose patter's a sad own goal

the nun with the e-vap ciggies who's trying to kick the habit
the Elvis Presley lookalike who's never caught a rabbit.

A man was caught badly scanning on the Underground today
but if you blinked, you missed it.

Cannahelpit in December Fog

[Cannahelpit is the most frequently nominated town in the annual 'Carboot Award' for the most dismal place to live.]

[Some unkind people may say that this is the best way to see Cannahelpit...]

[This page is also especially for those who appreciate the use of white space in poetry. And for lovers of modern art please re-imagine this space as 'The Quest for Identity in 21st Century Megacities aka Everyone's a Blank Canvas'.]

Exit Erinaceus (The Dark Highway)

[The community of Gaelic speakers is dwindling. As part of the drive to try to preserve the language, a new TV drama series in Gaelic is being filmed on location in Bannockpace.]

A dead hedgehog is dead
in any language.

No dignity in dying
for our awkward little cousin,
victim of circumstance,
of badger, truck, and strimmer,
the lethal trap of innocent milk
and discarded can.

Here lies the dimwit
heuchter-teuchter,
silently sprawled in mockery
of his slow old-fashioned ways

grim statistic on the reaper's card,
the identification of the body
cold and formal, wrapped
in a language that long ago
lost its vocal chord.

Inside the hedgehog community
        the ancient lament drifts to the heavens
                like a runaway kite.

One more blade of grass is ripped
        from the beautiful lawn.

                Severed quills litter
                the road to extinction.

Seeds must be sown
                        and hedgehog highways built.

For so say the elders who cling
defiantly to the far-flung
diaspora of the clans

the grandfathers and grandmothers
who made it across the big divide
to new ground, re-created
the warmth and spirit of home

who still sing
their hedgehog songs
and tell their hedgehog tales
of bygone heroism
and name their children
Ruairidh or *Seònaid*
the old way.

In gardens and rural lands
for so they tell it
the hedgehogs are kindly creatures,
your friend, defeater of
earthworms and beetles,
much more interesting than
slug pellets

and the neighbourhood
would be a poorer place
without their lugubrious rhythm
and distinctive charm,
yet their neighbours insist
on a different pace.

Just another number
for the road sweeper
one less hedgehog-speaker
in a world of monoglot machines,
dumped and left
like an old brown brush.

And The Sky Tumbled Down

[A news report that funding for Cancer research is down on last year.]

Wasted to bone and stranded
marble black eyes
nulled to void
prone and helpless
as a defeated gazelle
on the stone-cold earth.

An alien croak distorting voice
spirit sunken as a grave
each hallowed visit become
a vigil for breath
kith and kin framing silent eulogies
behind bravura smiles.

Deep in the crumbling interior
in a microscopic nether world
mutant gangsters swagger
like delinquent lions
ransacking sacred temples
replicating with indecent haste.

Overhead in the fractured light
a white-backed vulture, circling.

Waiting Rooms

[The future of the National Health service under review.]

The spider hangs by a thread in the waiting-room,
patiently exploring his insect queues,
assessing the injured and the ailing,
observed by strangers unwilling to engage
in conversation beyond spiders the weather
and heart attack, the clock ticking forward but time
drifting back in the flicking of old magazines.

The spinster waits quietly in the terminal hall,
crossword left with unanswered clues,
sipping espresso a whiff of bygone glamour,
passed by day-trippers unwilling to embrace
a thought beyond the coffee the pies and
the sandwich crust, the service on time but love
turned to dust like a faded perfume.

The fireman gasps for breath in the rubble,
deaf to the clamour of the worldwide news,
trapped with the dead and the dying,
sought by strangers unwilling to accept
the silence beyond the knock the cry or
the whistle peep, the clock ticking fast, but hope
burning deep until the last man is down.

Preserving the Countryside

[Extreme right-wing groups rioting.]

He's as bold as a highwayman, the urban fox,
No fear of lurking danger, the hungry
Nocturnal bandit slipping tenderfoot
Through the brightly-lit High Street,
Crowded with beer drinkers
Mad as dogs let loose on the trail
Making their loud empty barking noises.

Trotting instinctively towards richer pickings,
The lone raider of butchers' bins,
Quick, brown, one jump ahead,
Refuses the typecast role,
Confident of his own agenda,
Reckless even, too busy to notice
The furrier's window
Or the blazing red warning
In the gentlemen's outfitters.

Then up goes the cry, he's sighted,
The mob closes, blood is spilt,
The band of brothers certain that
There is no place for his kind
In this town, snarling deportation
Back to the country where he belongs,
The dirty thieving renegade.

Inner City Knight School

[A report on the lack of sports facilities for inner city kids.]

Metro evening - the sodium explodes
shattering glass to barbs
like arrows showering a battlefield.

    At street lamp number four,
    halfway to hell, torrential rain
    pummels the hill, the manhole cover
    spouts hot coals, paving slabs
    thud like a fortress wall,
    sinews stretch on a mediaeval rack.

        His saturated tracksuit heavy
        as armour plate, the lone runner
        curses time and blames his luck,
        spitting and yelling to shield
        the pain, a knight alone in his quest
        to face the thousand longknives.

Arms pumping iron in a flurry
of dust and flying rubble,
deafened by the city road's

    clamour of indifference, charging up the slope
    fired like St. George confronting
    his dragons, he suddenly senses
    another runner alongside,
    effortless and calm, matching strides
    then vanishing in the hurl of a spit.

        Fisting swords of dynamite,
        the warrior captures the hill
        and slams down the Flag of Defiance,
        lancing the sodden earth
        to mark the thin line
        between defeat and victory.

Festival of Raw Words

[A new international festival of poetry is launched at the Baycombe Arena, a venue better known for hosting boxing and MMA events.]

Poetry is a steel cage of raw conviction
        where fact gets into a fight with fiction
        trading words not punches or guns for hire
        scrapping for its life with its back to the wire

Let it be a pyrotechnic celebration
        soar on the thermals of imagination

Let it sing out loud like a Sunday bell
        put the jingle in the dingle of the Dingley Dell

Let it be the concrete at the base of the tallest tower
        rhapsodise about love but not the love of power

Let its union of words strike fear into corporate despots
        unravel the lies and untangle the knots

Let it be a priest on the banks of the silvery Tay
        let it glow like a candle in this ever-darkening day

Let a poem be my dog, let me take it for a walk
        let it off the leash and see if it can talk.

Square World

[A report has been published about low levels of literacy.]

The black crow flies to the sun
        and melts
like a tar-feathered Icarus
        and falls
into the deep
uncharted ocean

where press-ganged sailors
live in fear
        of the razor edge
        of the azure ledge
        and the sleeping Kraken.

Which tale foretells of dark misfortune,
according to the legend, for it is said:

        the square world cannot
                go round
                go round
        the spinning sun.

When you're only a landlubber
on the ship of life, watch out for
        the abyss
at the end of your day.

But remember the words of the ancient saying:

        The fish that never leaves the pond
        will never know what lies beyond.

Maybe in time you'll swim with the dolphins.

Dance of the Fireweeds

[A volcano has erupted, bringing terrible devastation.]

Krakatoa-Kaleido-Quake
Sulfuro-Tox
Tidehurler-Earthsplitter
Nuclear-Cloudspitter

Hellfire-Stonebreaker
Sky-Scorching-Rocks

The deer never bolted, the birds never flew,
dust in the stratosphere burnt the Sun blue.

Buffeting swirls of hot ashen smoke
mountain devouring mountain

plummeting smog in smothering choke
pyroclast magmatic fountain.

Tamarind and mango bark-stripped
and gnarled to splintery shards

bridges rock-mangled and ripped
lighthouses battered and scarred.

Billowing cornfields flat lava-rolled
villages stamped tephra black

demon-struck churches sermons untold
islanders dead in their track.

The bells never sounded, the geese never fled,
flames in the troposphere burned the Sky red.

In the eerie stillness of the afterlight
nursed in the cinders
tangled and defiant
one precious little seed
a flare in the fog of the powdered ash grey

a solitary fragile burning-pink fireweed.

Shooting For Fame

[Another senseless gun massacre in the USA. The usual outcry and the usual response, but no real change. The USA continues to top the leaderboard for guns held per capita, allegedly well over 300 million in total.]

were the honey bees too plain ?
or the cherry trees mundane ?
      were you never in awe of a mountain ?

were the lawns too green ?
or the dawns routine ?
      did you never draw breath from a fountain ?

            was the sunshine not enough for you ?
                  did the sun not kiss your face ?

were the cars too stacked ?
or the bars too packed ?
      did you never want to go cast a reel ?

was the day too slow ?
or the pay too low?
      did you never try to cut a new deal ?

            was the rainfall not enough for you ?
                  did the rain not kiss your face ?

was the firefly not disarming ?
was the child's cry not alarming ?
      did you dwell in a never-never zone ?

were the tarot cards not aligned ?
did the shadows eclipse your mind ?
      did you never just go skim a stone ?

            was the moonlight not enough for you ?
                  did the stars not give you space ?

Saturday Night at The Ritz

[Nervous times as political leaders around the world grow ever more confrontational and undemocratic in their actions.]

Razzle Dazzle 1976

Claustrophobia and stench were part of the attraction
in the shadowy crypt of damp walls,
the bricked-up wishing well
of broken hearts they called The Ritz,
our regular haunt for some sweaty hands-on action.

We'd queue round the block for the privilege,
adrenalin and booze on tap in a lethal
mix, the girls dressed to kill in stiletto heels,
the neon-fuelled buzz from the loose-wired circuit
giving Saturday night an extra edge.

Cocksure as kings we'd laugh and joke
oblivious to the spillages and the vomit
and the legless zombies trodden on like bugs
in the reeking corners of the bombed-out bogs
high on the fumes of crazy smoke.

We'd jump to the thump of the music with sex-mad
nurses swapping ciggies and banter and spit,
lost in the red mist of alcohol, the taxi money blown to hell,
then scramble out for air through the crowded hall,
burning our bridges with every spark that we had.

Lamplight 1916

Ratto, Tommy and Jock had been lodged at The Ritz,
candlelit apartments perfumed with roses and peppermint,
after catching the C-in-C's breezy announcement
that it would be a jolly good show and they'd share a case
of beer after settling their account with cousin Fritz.

Keen as mustard, the pals lined up, bright-eyed young men,
the old general gave them a lift to their dandy new base,
and with dandy suits and dandy boots out they stepped,
the fireworks whizzed all around, the music never stopped,
and they partied all night like it was 1899 all over again.

Halloween was the theme, it was all the rage.
They put on masks in a race with the other guests,
and joined in a parlour game called 'Ghosts'
where Fritz burst balloons in Tommy's face,
and it seemed like all the world was their stage.

Jumping like frogs they charged around half mad,
threw each other silver balls in a crazy chase,
bathed in the mud springs then danced down
the hall and sang a last song at the break of dawn.
What a gas, what a time they had !

Illuminations 2036

The war to end all wars has ended. The stars have fled
the sky, day is night and the moon's a burst balloon.
Bullets of black carbon rain down on the ghost town,
the dust of fairgrounds and seaside hotels long forgotten
in a landscape from Mars smoking eerily red.

Wolves sniff around the corpses of legless dolls
in the Arctic coldness of broken hearts and unheard tunes,
howling victims in a tragedy instigated by comedy excess,
missing the post-apocalypse irony - no more bills or taxes
no traffic jams, no strikes, no binges on drugs or alcohol.

Toxic fumes of sulphur make no distinction,
the bunkers won't bail the oligarchs nor will their masks.
Rubble has no religion - the churches synagogues mosques
too late for prayer. Cavemen jump to the thump of new elites.
Lines of zombies lurch down the path to total extinction.

Nothing grows in the After-Earth's putrid layers of slime.
All the circuits are blown to hell in a planet numb with fear.
Crazy shadows dance around stuttering camp fires
in the lonely corners and haunted crypts of the bombed-out streets.
Our past, their future, lost in the dark hole of time.

Soundbite City Blues

Good Night, Mr Robert,
Good Night, Sir John.

She looks busy, the cleaning lady
dusting and hoovering
the corners of her world
not her world
not noticing the absence of ashtrays
nor the smoking gun nor the
trigger-pull of ratings just bins
now full of disks with
labels like bullets

- third-world poverty
- landmine atrocity
- religious extremity
- political expediency

muttering routinely to herself
in an unreported language
in the unreported place
of a story that is dead
or never was.

Pity the cry of the wasted and canned,
cast to the wind, heading for dumbdown
into coasters and windchimes.
She collects these scraps
for her nephew, he says
trash bins are ripe fruit
for the scavengers of the night.
She doesn't understand his fancy words,
goes outside, lights one up.

Marble

Poetry is sculpture with words
and in the space between the words

in the projection of volume and light
and surface and colour

in its manifold perspectives of form
in its contours of language and style

and its crafting of the invisible
its definition of the indefinable

the meaning hides behind the wall
the art waits quietly alone in the hall.

ACKNOWLEDGEMENTS

The following poems have achieved recognition in UK poetry competitions (some versions in this book have minor improvements over the originals):

Camomile Tea
(1st prize, Buxton Poetry Competition, 2017)

The Putter-Togetherers
(3rd prize, Southport Poetry Competition, 2016)

A Million Suns
(Highly Commended, Wirral Festival of Firsts, 2015)

Parades in London (winter)
(Commended, as *'Pavement from inside Costa Coffee King's Cross'*, Yeovil Poetry Competition, 2018)

Hang-Gliding
(Longlisted (top 17), Yeovil Poetry Competition, 2015)

Speed Dating in a Northern Town
(Longlisted, Bedford Poetry Competition, 2019)

The following mixed-style works have achieved recognition in the Yeovil 'Writing Without Restrictions' competition:

Baycombe (entered as *'Blackpoolium'*)
(Highly Commended, 2018)

Soundbite City News
(Commended, 2016)

Both versions here have extensive additional new material.

Some of the poems also appear on **www.burg34.com**.

NOTES

Bannockpace and *Cannahelpit* are my fictional Scottish towns. *Baycombe* is a fictional English seaside resort, and *Bhagranapur* is a fictional Indian village.
Any similarity to any real locations or persons would be coincidental.

www.ingramcontent.com/pod-product-compliance
Ingram Content Group UK Ltd.
Pitfield, Milton Keynes, MK11 3LW, UK
UKHW020135250726
13967UKWH00002B/676